SHORT WALKS IN PEMBROKESHIRE – TENBY AND THE SOUTH

by Dennis and Jan Kelsall

Leaving the beach at Amroth (Walk 1)

CONTENTS

Using this guide 4
Route summary table 6
Map key 7
Introduction 9
  Walking in Pembrokeshire 10
  A good time to visit... 10
  Where to make a base 11
  Getting around 11

The walks
1. Amroth, Pleasant Valley and Colby 13
2. Saundersfoot and Monkstone Beach 19
3. Tenby 23
4. Church Doors and Lydstep Point 27
5. Manorbier 33
6. Stackpole Quay, Barafundle Bay and the Lily Ponds .. 37
7. Bosherston Lily Ponds 43
8. St Govan's Head 47
9. The Green Bridge and Bullslaughter Bay 53
10. West Angle 59
11. Carew Castle 65
12. St Ishmael's 69
13. The Dale Peninsula 73
14. Runwayskiln and Marloes Sands 79
15. Wooltack Point 83

Useful information 87

USING THIS GUIDE

Routes in this book

In this book you will find a selection of easy or moderate walks suitable for almost everyone, including casual walkers and families with children, or for when you only have a short time to fill. The routes have been carefully chosen to allow you to explore the area and its attractions. Most routes are circular, although some walks are there-and-back. Although there may be some climbs there is no challenging terrain, but do bear in mind that conditions can sometimes be wet or muddy underfoot. A route summary table is included on page 6 to help you choose the right walk.

Clothing and footwear

You won't need any special equipment to enjoy these walks. The weather in Britain can be changeable, so choose clothing suitable for the season and wear or carry a waterproof jacket. For footwear, comfortable walking boots or trainers with a good grip are best. A small rucksack for drinks, snacks and spare clothing is useful. See www.adventuresmart.uk.

Walk descriptions

At the beginning of each walk you'll find all the information you need:

- start/finish location, with postcode and a what3words address to help you find it
- parking and transport information, estimated walking time, total distance and climb
- details of public toilets available along the route and where you can get refreshments
- a summary of the key highlights of the walk and what you might see

Timings given are the time to complete the walk at a reasonable walking pace. Allow extra time for extended stops or if walking with children.

The route is described in clear, easy-to-follow directions, with each waypoint marked on an accompanying map extract. It's a good idea to read the whole of the route instructions before setting out, so that you know what to expect.

Maps, GPX files and what3words

Extracts from the OS® 1:25,000 map accompany each route. GPX files for all the walks in this book are available to download at www.cicerone.co.uk/1175/gpx.

What3words is a free smartphone app which identifies every 3m square of the globe with a unique three-word address, e.g. ///destiny.cafe.sonic. For more information see https://what3words.com/products/what3words-app.

USING THIS GUIDE

Walking with children

Even young children can be surprisingly strong walkers, but every family is different and you may need to adapt the timings given in this book to take that into account. Make sure you go at the pace of the slowest member and choose a walk with an exciting objective in mind, such as a cave, river, waterfall or picnic spot. Many of the walks can be shortened to suit – suggestions are included at the end of the route description.

Dogs

Sheep or cattle may be found grazing on a number of these walks. Keep dogs under control at all times so that they don't scare or disturb livestock or wildlife. Cattle, particularly cows with calves, may very occasionally pose a risk to walkers with dogs. If you ever feel threatened by cattle, you should let go of your dog's lead and let it run free.

Enjoying the countryside responsibly

Enjoy the countryside and treat it with respect to protect our natural environments. Stick to footpaths and take your litter home with you. When driving, slow down on rural roads and park considerately, or better still use public transport. For more details check out www.gov.uk/countryside-code.

The Countryside Code

Respect everyone
- be considerate to those living in, working in and enjoying the countryside
- leave gates and property as you find them
- do not block access to gateways or driveways when parking
- be nice, say hello, share the space
- follow local signs and keep to marked paths unless wider access is available

Protect the environment
- take your litter home – leave no trace of your visit
- do not light fires and only have BBQs where signs say you can
- always keep dogs under control and in sight
- dog poo – bag it and bin it – any public waste bin will do
- care for nature – do not cause damage or disturbance

Enjoy the outdoors
- check your route and local conditions
- plan your adventure – know what to expect and what you can do
- enjoy your visit, have fun, make a memory

SHORT WALKS PEMBROKESHIRE

ROUTE SUMMARY TABLE

WALK NAME	START POINT	TIME	DISTANCE
1. Amroth, Pleasant Valley and Colby	Amroth main car park	2½hr	7.5km (4¾ miles)
2. Saundersfoot and Monkstone Beach	Saundersfoot harbour slipway	2¼hr	5km (3 miles)
3. Tenby	Tenby South Beach	1hr	3km (2 miles)
4. Church Doors and Lydstep Point	Manorbier Youth Hostel	1¾hr	4km (2½ miles)
5. Manorbier	Manorbier Beach car park	1½hr	4km (2½ miles)
6. Stackpole Quay, Barafundle Bay and the Lily Ponds	Stackpole Quay car park	2¾hr	8km (5 miles)
7. Bosherston Lily Ponds	Bosherston Lily Ponds car park	1hr	3km (1¾ miles)
8. St Govan's Head	Broad Haven Beach South car park	2½hr	7.5km (4¾ miles)
9. The Green Bridge and Bullslaughter Bay	Stack Rocks car park	2¾hr	7km (4¼ miles)
10. West Angle	West Angle Beach car park	2hr	6km (3¾ miles)
11. Carew Castle	Carew Castle car park	½hr	1.5km (1 mile)
12. St Ishmael's	St Ishmael's sports field	1½hr	4km (2½ miles)
13. The Dale Peninsula	Dale Beach car park	4hr	11km (6¾ miles)
14. Runwayskiln and Marloes Sands	Runwayskiln car park	1½hr	4km (2½ miles)
15. Wooltack Point	Martin's Haven car park	1¼hr	3km (2 miles)

MAP KEY

HIGHLIGHTS
Beaches, woodland and a formal garden
Harbour, beaches, cliff-top views and woodland
Town trail, churches and museums
Beach, cliff-top views and spectacular formations
Castle, dolmen, cliff-top views and unusual formations
Cliff-top views, formations, beaches and lily ponds
Lily ponds, woodland and beach
Cliff-top views, formations and tiny chapel
Cliff-top views, formations and Iron Age fort
Beach, Napoleonic forts, lifeboat stations and estuary views
Castle, tidal mill and Celtic cross
Estuary views, beaches, Victorian folly and country church
Coastal views, beaches, Napoleonic forts and lighthouses
Cliff-top views, shipwreck, Iron Age fort and beach
Coastal views, beach and island boat trips

SYMBOLS USED ON ROUTE MAPS

S — Start point

F — Finish point

SF — Start and finish at the same place

4→ — Waypoint

~ — Route line

~ — Alternative route line

MAPPING IS SHOWN AT A SCALE OF 1:25,000

0 KM — 0.25 — 0.5
0 miles — 0.25

DOWNLOAD THE GPX FILES FOR FREE AT
www.cicerone.co.uk/1175/GPX

Across Tenby Harbour to Castle Hill (Walk 3)

INTRODUCTION

Looking towards Long Matthew Point (Walk 8)

Pointing towards the Atlantic Ocean and the setting sun, the ragged Pembrokeshire peninsula is the south-westernmost tip of Wales. With a much-convoluted 300km coastline, it is intimately connected with the sea, which has brought people, ideas and trade since the earliest times. Although predominantly rural, it has been no neglected backwater. Fleeting traces show that hunter gatherers arrived soon after the last glacial period, with more tangible remains in the form of dolmens, defended settlements and field systems left by those who came later to settle and farm the land. Close links with Brittany and Ireland allowed the spread of Celtic Christianity, but the sea also brought the Vikings. Later on, the Norman invasion swept through southern Pembrokeshire leaving a scattering of castles, while the first Tudor king, Henry VII, was born at Pembroke Castle. Harbours, coves and inlets provided landings for trade, passengers and fishing, while wars and conflict made their mark on the landscape too. Such a rich history has left much across the landscape that remains visible, which, coupled with a native passion for storytelling, legend and song, means that almost everywhere, there are things to explore or ponder.

Walking in Pembrokeshire

The 15 walks in this book have been chosen to highlight the spectacular natural beauty of the area, where land and sea stand in hoary confrontation, with bastions of craggy cliffs rising behind sweeping bays and innumerable tiny coves separated by defiant promontories. In contrast, tidal estuaries and twisting rivers penetrate deep into the heartland, where steep-sided valleys and sloping woodlands climb to a gently undulating plateau. The countryside is chequered with a myriad of small fields and enclosures bound by herb-rich boundaries of stone, earth and hedge. Such dramatic beauty and an amazing abundance of wildlife, particularly in flowers, birds, insects and sea life, all contributed to the coast's designation as a National Park in 1952.

The climate is generally mild, with snow and ice along the coast being rare. Wind and rain however can occur at any time, but don't be put off; the ins and outs of endless bays can often mean that shelter is just around the corner, while Dale claims to be one of the sunniest spots in Wales. Much of the coast is rugged and, inevitably, there are ups and downs, but nowhere along the walks suggested here are the challenges overly great. Formal paths are generally clear and gradients usually short, while frequent pauses to admire the view give ample opportunity to catch one's breath. Navigation is rarely a problem either, just remember which side the sea is supposed to be on. Some words of warning though. Be very careful walking along cliffs, especially with children and dogs, particularly in wet or windy weather and do not attempt to clamber down to the shore except on recognised paths. Be aware too of the ever-changing tide, which can cut off small bays before reaching the main beach.

A good time to visit

Much of Pembrokeshire's coastal margin has escaped heavy cultivation and the sheer number and variety of wildflowers that burst forth in spring and summer is a sight

Looking into Bullslaughter Bay (Walk 9)

to behold. The same is often true of the hedges that border quiet lanes and the pockets of ancient woodland tucked into sheltered corners or narrow valleys. Spring and early summer is also the time when countless seabirds come to nest on the coastal cliffs, stacks and islands. The incessant noise of their calls can be deafening and there is a constant coming and going as they feed hungry chicks. Towards the end of summer is the time for seals to come ashore to birth their pups. They usually choose inaccessible coves to be safe from predators, flopping back and forth to the sea to mount guard or search for fish in the bay.

Where to make a base

In the south of the county, the area covered by this book, the main centres are Pembroke, Tenby and nearby Saundersfoot, all of which are served by rail from Newport and the wider National network, and act as excellent bases from which to explore the area. Accommodation can be found in many of the smaller villages too. There is a good selection of cafés, pubs and restaurants, many of which feature local produce and specialities, so you should not go hungry.

Getting around

As for getting about, limited local buses and a Flexi on-demand system operate within the area, but changes in provision and funding make it advisable to check routes and current timetables before setting out. There are several reliable local taxi firms operating too. All the walks are either circular or there-and-back routes and begin at or close to car parking.

Saundersfoot beach (Walk 2)

The summerhouse in Colby Gardens

WALK 1
Amroth, Pleasant Valley and Colby

Start/finish	Amroth main car park
Locate	SA67 8NG ///deferring.ticked.easy
Cafés/pubs	Pubs at Amroth and Wiseman's Bridge, cafés at Amroth and Colby Gardens
Transport	Limited bus service from Tenby
Parking	Car park at Amroth (pay-and-display) and on the street at Wiseman's Bridge
Toilets	On the promenade at Amroth and Wiseman's Bridge

Time 2½hr
Distance 7.5km (4¾ miles)
Climb 210m

A satisfying walk exploring two fine beaches, woodland, industrial heritage and the superb Colby Gardens

Take time to glance back for the best views during the first stretch of this walk, which links two splendid beaches before following the aptly named pleasant valley to an old iron works. A climb over Summerhill takes the walk to Colby, where a tearoom, walled garden and more woodland give a fitting finale to this ramble.

Looking east from the beach at Amroth

SHORT WALKS PEMBROKESHIRE

Wiseman's Bridge Inn

1 Exit the car park from the bottom-right corner, turn right to the coast and right again onto the promenade. At the end, look for the Coast Path leaving beside the toilets. It climbs steeply through trees onto the headland. The Pembrokeshire Coast Path runs for almost 300km (186 miles) from

The beach at Wiseman's Bridge

Amroth to St Dogmael's. Pass along a bracken meadow, turning through a gate onto a hedged path. To the left it rises over the crest of the hill, eventually broadening to a lane. Continue downhill, joining the main lane to regain the coast at **Wiseman's Bridge Inn**. Carry on beside the beach to a bridge at the far end.

2 At the bridge, climb steps and follow a narrow lane into **Pleasant Valley**. Approaching a cottage, bear off right along a track, the course of an old tramway that ran from the harbour at Saundersfoot. Stick with the main path, later re-crossing the stream and eventually emerging onto a lane beside the entrance to Heritage Holiday Park. Turn left in there to look at the former Kilgetty Iron Works.

3 Return to the lane and cross to **Mill House Caravan Park** opposite. Follow the drive ahead past the ablution block to a bend. Go forward between

Colby woodlands

caravans to a stile. Bear left uphill to a gap in the top wall and walk out to a narrow lane. Follow it right.

4 Reaching a sharp bend by cottages, bear off left on a track. After 30m, turn right to a stile from which a path rises across a wooded hillside. Over another stile, continue at the field edge to meet a hedged track. Follow it up to a bend and go ahead through a kissing gate along a tree-lined path to **Cwmrath Farm**. Join its access track out to a lane.

5 At the lane turn right, but then take the first left along a bridleway down to another farm. Where the track swings into the yard, keep ahead on a descending path into a wooded valley. Ignoring paths off, wind down to a junction at the bottom. Walk ahead past a small building and over a stream to emerge onto another lane.

6 Turn right past Colby Lodge and then turn in at the entrance to **Colby Woodland Garden**. Beyond the tearoom and ticket office, the track meanders pleasantly along the delightful Colby Valley. Eventually reaching cottages, it emerges onto a lane that leads back down to the car park in Amroth.

– To shorten

For a shorter walk of 3km (1hr), park at Wiseman's Bridge and simply follow the old tramway path there and back to the ironworks.

Colby Gardens

The valley had long been mined for coal, but the arrival of John Colby towards the end of the 18th century set things on an industrial scale. Although his venture was highly profitable, the seams were worked out within 30 years and Colby sold the estate to Samuel Kay, a Stockport pharmacist. He began the valley's transformation into a woodland garden, his daughter subsequently laying out the formal gardens. The unique summerhouse in the walled garden is, however, a relative newcomer, dating from 1976 and decorated inside with a fine trompe l'oeil (a painting that creates the illusion of a real scene).

Hedge banks cloaked in purple thrift

WALK 2
Saundersfoot and Monkstone Beach

Time 2¼hr
Distance 5km (3 miles)
Climb 220m

Start/finish	*Saundersfoot harbour slipway*
Locate	*SA69 9HE ///stung.stress.shortens*
Cafés/pubs	*Cafés and pubs in Saundersfoot*
Transport	*Limited bus service from Tenby*
Parking	*Car park at harbour (pay-and-display)*
Toilets	*At harbour*

A popular holiday resort, Saundersfoot is the base for this coastal woodland walk to Monkstone Beach

A there-and-back walk from the lively harbour at Saundersfoot, the route rises over wooded cliffs to Monkstone Point. There is an optional detour around the headland, while Monkstone's sheltered beach is tucked below and reached by a good, albeit steep, stepped path. The state of the tide can govern how you begin and end the walk, so check tide tables before setting out.

On the beach below Rhode Wood, looking back to Saundersfoot

1 At low tide, you can begin along the beach beside the harbour. From the top of the slipway, walk around the back of the harbour. Swing left past toilets along the southern quay to the corner, where a ramp winds down to the beach. Go right for about 200m and then leave up a stepped path to emerge onto the bend of a street. Alternatively, if the tide is in, from the harbour walk out to the main road and go left. Follow it up, left and right through a couple of bends. After the road levels, turn off left along The Glen and head down to a bend at the bottom.

2 At the bend look for the Coast Path signed off left beside a gate into **Rhode Wood**. The way twists up

The harbour at Saundersfoot

through old oak woodland, occasionally breaking out at the edge of the cliffs to give panoramic views across Carmarthen Bay. Before long, the way descends to a junction at the base of a valley, where a path off sharp left leads to the shore.

> The woods beside the path hide old quarries, coal pits and a lime kiln (look for it beside the path as you climb from Waypoint 3)

3 However, remain with the waymarked Coast Path, which bears left over a plank bridge to climb back onto the cliffs. Through a gate at the top, the way runs briefly at the edge of fields before returning to trees. Carry on to a waymarked junction behind **Monkstone Point**.

4 The more direct Coast Path is signed to the right across the neck, while ahead a detour around the headland can be taken returning along its southern flank. Either way will do, as the paths come together again a little further on.

5 Once the paths rejoin, a signpost indicates a steep, stepped path that zigzags down to **Monkstone Beach**.

6 The return to Saundersfoot simply reverses your outward route. However,

Monkstone Beach and point

the changing tide may have revealed or covered the beach beside the harbour, thus perhaps necessitating a change of route back to the car park.

> **— To shorten**
> Simply walk (3km, 1hr) as far as the valley below Trevayne Wood (Waypoint 3) and drop to the beach there. At low tide, you can walk back to Saundersfoot along the shore.

Saundersfoot

From a tiny fishing village where boats were unloaded on the sands at low tide, Saundersfoot grew to an industrial port in the 19th century. A steam tramway connected the mines and iron works to a purpose-built harbour, the final section of track running along the high street right onto the quayside. At its peak, over 100,000 tons of coal a year left for places as far afield as Hong Kong. But with the dawning 20th century, the heyday passed; local mines became worked out and the harbour unable to accommodate increasingly large ships. However, the town reinvented itself as a holiday resort and remains as popular as ever.

WALK 3
Tenby

Start/finish	Tenby South Beach
Locate	SA70 7EL ///costumes.intricate.acrobat
Cafés/pubs	Pubs and cafés in Tenby
Transport	Rail and bus services to Tenby
Parking	Car park at South Beach (pay-and-display)
Toilets	At South Beach car park and above Castle Beach

Time 1hr
Distance 3km (2 miles)
Climb 60m

A strategic port since the days of the Vikings, Tenby is well worth exploring on this gentle town centre walk

This interesting trail wanders through the old town, onto the harbour and around Castle Hill, seeking corners that reflect Tenby's intriguing past. Amongst the places you might visit are St Mary's Church, the Merchant's House, the town museum and St Catherine's Island fort (at low tide), or you can simply bask in the ambience of this lively, yet unspoiled resort.

Low tide in Tenby Harbour

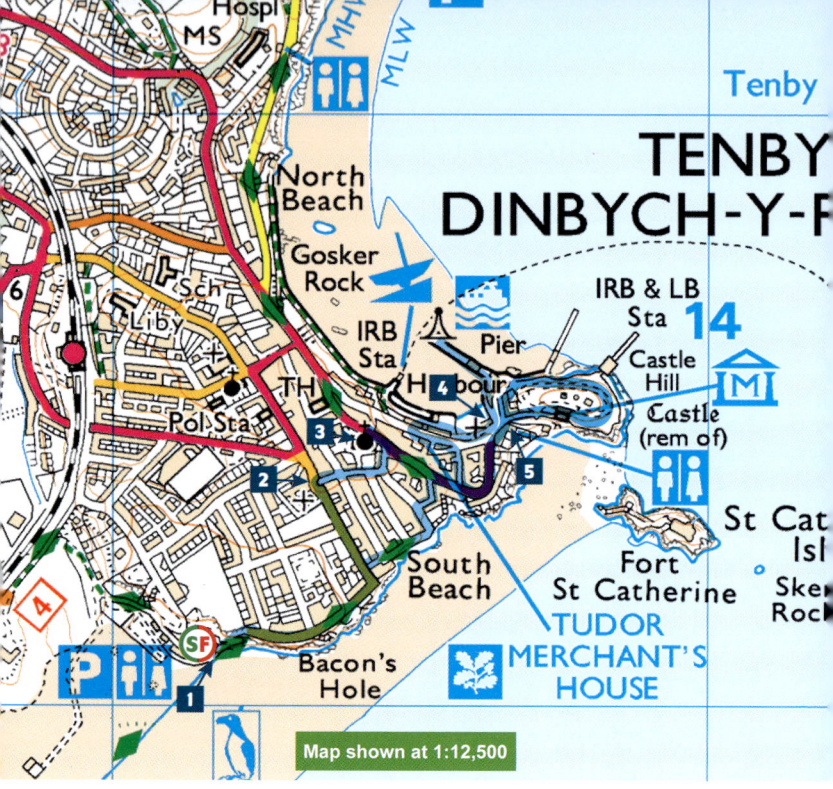

Map shown at 1:12,500

1 Leave the lower end of the car park, following a walkway to the left past a beach bar. Climb beyond around a sharp bend to a junction and head right, following a sign to the Town Centre. Joining the Esplanade, walk to its far end and go left along St Florence Parade beside the town walls to Five Arches Gate.

2 Pass through the gate and head along St George's Street and continue past St Mary's churchyard. At the end, bear left to emerge on St Julian's Street. The entrance to St Mary's Church is then to the left.

3 Leaving the church, walk back past the junction and continue to reach the Lifeboat Tavern. There turn left, passing between a pair of post boxes, one of which is Victorian. The narrow passage, Quay Hill, cuts through by the National Trust's Tudor Merchant's House to emerge on Crackwell Street. Go left a short distance then turn back

Tenby Old Lifeboat Station

right down steps to reach a small quay behind the **harbour**. Walk forward, passing the tiny St Julian's Chapel and the former Seamen's Mission to a junction.

4 Go left at the junction. Branching left again takes you onto the **pier**, while the right fork leads past Laston House (Tenby's first seawater baths) to Castle Hill. Carry on past Tenby's former and present **lifeboat stations**. From the pavilion, there is a view of the Victorian fort on St Catherine's Island, while behind on top of the hill are the Coastguard House, the remains of the castle and the Albert Memorial. Leave past the Museum and Art Gallery, walking down to the foot of Castle Hill.

5 If the tide is out, you can then turn sharp left through the arch to the beach. St Catherine's Island and fort lie opposite or you can simply follow the shore below the town back to South Beach car park. At high tide, bear left and then keep left along St Julian's Street. After 200m, turn left again into Cobb Lane. At the far end, go left on Cresswell Street, swinging right along The Paragon. At the end, dogleg around the Imperial Hotel to regain the Esplanade and retrace your outward steps back to the car park.

> ⓘ Begun in 1867, St Catherine's Fort was part of the Royal Dockyard defences, to deter Napoleon from landing and striking overland to Pembroke Dock

St Catherine's Island

Tenby

Early Tenby prospered on fishing and trade, its sheltered harbour a gateway to the Bristol Channel, Ireland and the Continent. The Normans made it a stronghold and its harbour and defences were improved over the centuries, first against the Welsh, subsequently for the Tudors during the Wars of the Roses and then later to meet the threat of Spanish invasion. Tenby flourished until Cromwell seized the town in 1648, with the plague striking two years later. There followed 150 years of decline, arrested only when Napoleon threw Europe into chaos. Denied their Grand Tours, the gentry turned to the 'staycation' and local entrepreneur Sir William Paxton began redeveloping the town as a genteel seaside spa.

> ⓘ *Tenby's Welsh name, Dinbych-y-pysgod, means 'little fort of the fish'*

WALK 4
Church Doors and Lydstep Point

Start/finish	*Manorbier Youth Hostel*
Locate	*SA70 7TT ///dining.cluttered.steer*
Cafés/pubs	*Café at youth hostel*
Transport	*No public transport*
Parking	*Car park at youth hostel*
Toilets	*No public toilets available*

Time 1¾hr
Distance 4km (2½ miles)
Climb 180m

Spectacular cliff formations are compelling features of this stunning section of coast

Head almost anywhere along the Pembrokeshire coast and you will find the cliff-top scenery stunning. This walk above Church Doors to Lydstep Point is no exception; erosion of the vertical rock strata has created an impressive 'through cave' at Church Doors and left awesomely sheer cliffs backing tiny coves on the adjacent Lydstep headland.

Church Doors beach

Looking into the Draught

WALK 4 – CHURCH DOORS AND LYDSTEP POINT

1 Leave the bottom end of the car park and follow a path straight out towards the coast. At the end, go left to meet the coast above a steep flight of steps down to the cove at Church Doors. It is then worth briefly going right above **Skrinkle Haven** for the view across the bay.

2 Return to the top of the steps and continue onwards along the Coast Path, which meanders around a series of small inaccessible coves cut into the cliffs. Before long, the path winds downwards to cross a deep fold above the head of a narrow cove, the Draught. Look across to see a massive collapsed blowhole, it is connected to the sea by a cave, which is said to have been used by smugglers. You can reach the beach and caves by turning right at the bottom. Otherwise, bear left, climbing strenuously to a gate at the top.

The tiny coves below the Lydstep promontory are known as Mother Carey's Kitchen. To sailors, Mother Carey is a malignant personification of stormy seas, and the surging waves that endlessly batter the base of the cliffs can certainly live up to that image.

3 Immediately through the gate, take a path off on the right that leads back to the coast, passing above the blowhole seen earlier and on to the tip of **Lydstep Point**. The northern face of Lydstep Head was extensively quarried for its limestone. Carry on around the perimeter of the headland, eventually reaching a small car park.

4 Walk through the car park and leave towards the far end through a gate on the left. At an immediate crosspath, go right and then right again to return to the top of the steep steps climbed on the way out (Waypoint 3). Follow them down and head back along your outward route to the youth hostel car park.

— To shorten

If the tide is out, you may wish to spend all day on the beach at Church Doors (1.5km, 30min).

View east from Skomar

✚ To lengthen

Walk out from the small car park on Lydstep Point to the lane and follow it right, downhill to Lydstep's kilometre-long beach, extension adds 1.5km (30min).

Church Doors and Skrinkle Haven

Access to the bouldery cove at Church Doors is via a steep flight of steps, and when the tide is out you can stand beneath the awesome 'door' that has been cut through a stubby promontory. The beach at Skrinkle Haven is an altogether different prospect, the only approach (other than by boat) is through a narrow cave piercing the headland separating it from Church Doors. Have a look, but be very careful if you venture through. The passage is available only for a short time either side of low tide before rising waters quickly block the return route. Be warned.

The cliffs by Presipe Bay

WALK 5
Manorbier

Start/finish	Manorbier Beach car park
Locate	SA70 7SY ///glider.cheetahs.hidden
Cafés/pubs	Tea room and pub in Manorbier
Transport	Bus service from Haverfordwest
Parking	Car park at Manorbier beach (pay-and-display)
Toilets	At Manorbier beach

The path gently gains height along low cliffs behind Manorbier's beach and around Priest's Nose, later dipping across a fold to round a small promontory overlooking Presipe Bay. Leaving the coast, the way climbs inland to Hill Farm, picking up a track beyond that leads to the village, where there is both a tea shop and pub. The final stretch follows the lane beneath the walls of Manorbier Castle.

Time 1½hr
Distance 4km (2½ miles)
Climb 170m

A circular ramble featuring a Stone Age dolmen, unusual cliff formations and an impressive castle

Manorbier Castle from behind the beach

1 A path from the bottom of the car park leads towards the coast. Bear left around the head of the beach, joining the Coast Path, leading up a stepped path at the far end. Climb away above low, sloping cliffs, shortly reaching the **King's Quoit** dolmen.

> The King's Quoit is a Neolithic chamber dated to around 3000BC, a massive capstone once supported on three upright stones, one of which has since fallen. Although generally regarded as burial monuments, the specific purpose of dolmens remain a mystery.

2 The Coast Path continues around **Priest's Nose**, passing behind a zawn, a dramatically narrow chasm that falls sheer to the sea, so amazingly precise that it could have been cut by a gigantic saw. There is another gash a little further along, but being wider is less sensational. Around the point, the path carries on above a steepening grassy slope that falls to low, bare sandstone cliffs, later tucking behind inaccessible coves. After gaining height onto a small headland, the cliffs turn in above **Presipe Bay** and continue until reaching a gate.

3 Pass through the gate, but immediately abandon the Coast Path to follow a path climbing away beside a stone wall and then a fence. Through another gate continue over the hill in the next field. Towards the bottom, swing right parallel to the boundary and leave through a gate. Bear left, skirting the buildings of **Hill Farm** to another gate.

WALK 5 – MANORBIER

The King's Quoit dolmen

However, cross the nearby stile instead, and head directly away across successive fields. Exit the bottom of the third field over a stile onto a rough track by an overgrown lime kiln.

4 Go left, shortly joining a narrow lane. Follow it ahead, eventually reaching the main lane at the edge of **Manorbier** village.

5 The tea room and pub lie just to the right while the way back is down to the left, passing beneath the **Manorbier Castle** walls, to the car park. A short detour left, partway down the hill, will take you to the Church of St James the Great on the other side of the valley.

> ⓘ *A wartime airfield at Manorbier housed an anti-aircraft gunnery school, with pilot-less planes being used as targets*

> **– To shorten**
>
> Follow the Coast Path only as far as the King's Quoit dolmen, perhaps spending the rest of the day on Manorbier's fine beach, shortening the walk to 1.5km (30min).

+ To lengthen

Shortly before reaching the gate and turn-off to Hill Farm at Waypoint 3, a stepped path off on the right leads down to the beach at Presipe Bay adding 0.75km (30min).

Manorbier Castle

Manorbier Castle was begun at the end of the 11th century by Otto de Barri, one of the knights accompanying William the Conqueror in the invasion of Britain. From a simple motte and bailey on the tip of a spur overlooking the sheltered bay, it was soon extended in stone to create an impressive fortification. But, apart from a minor assault in 1327 over family succession, the castle saw no action and many of the defensive slits gave way to windows. The end came after being taken and slighted by Cromwell's forces in the Civil War when it was largely abandoned until restoration began during the 19th century.

Manorbier Bay

WALK 6
Stackpole Quay, Barafundle Bay and the Lily Ponds

Start/finish	*Stackpole Quay car park*
Locate	*SA71 5LS ///restored.blows.quoted*
Cafés/pubs	*Tearoom at Stackpole Quay*
Transport	*Limited bus service from Pembroke Dock*
Parking	*National Trust car park at Stackpole Quay (pay-and-display)*
Toilets	*At Stackpole Quay car park*

Time 2¾hr
Distance 8km (5 miles)
Climb 165m

An exciting cliff-top walk linking sheltered beaches and the famous Bosherston Lily Ponds

Although a longer walk, it is not demanding, with only a couple of short uphill stretches along the way. The cliff-top views are spectacular and contrast with the wooded shores of the Bosherston lakes passed later on, while the final return follows a good track across the fields. There is usually wildlife to see, both from the cliffs and by the lakes, so keep your eyes open.

Stackpool Quay

Sea stack below Mowingword

WALK 6 – STACKPOLE QUAY, BARAFUNDLE BAY AND THE LILY PONDS

1 Begin along a path leaving to the right of the car park information cabin, passing behind the Boathouse Café to a junction. Left drops to Stackpole's stony beach, while ahead, a viewpoint overlooks the tiny harbour.

The picturesque harbour of Stackpole Quay was built at the end of the 18th century and used to land coal and other supplies for the Stackpole Estate as well as providing a berth for Lord Cawdor's pleasure yacht, the Speedwich.

39

SHORT WALKS PEMBROKESHIRE

Barafundle beach

2 The walk, however, takes the stepped path off right to Barafundle. Emerging onto a grassy headland, the main path cuts straight ahead, although the best views are from a cliff-top path. The path eventually dips to an arched stone gateway above **Barafundle Bay**, marking the top of steps down to the lovely beach.

3 Walk across the sand (keeping by the dunes at high tide) and climb away at the far side through a copse of sycamore trees. Back on high ground, follow the cliff path out to **Stackpole Head**, occasionally looking back to

Stackpole Head

WALK 6 – STACKPOLE QUAY, BARAFUNDLE BAY AND THE LILY PONDS

Approaching Bosherston Lily Ponds

see the natural arches of Griffith Lorts Hole.

4 From Stackpole Head the path swings back along the southern edge of the headland, cutting across the spur of Mowingword and behind an inaccessible bay, dramatically littered with sea stacks and fallen rocks. Carry on past a striking zawn (a deep, narrow sea inlet), an impressive blowhole and a sandy cove. Eventually rounding **Saddle Point**, the path turns inland above Broad Haven beach to a kissing gate at the edge of sand dunes.

5 Once through the gate take the onward path above low cliffs, shortly closing in on a stone wall. Keep ahead in the dunes, soon dropping to a 'T' junction at the foot of the ponds.

6 The path left leads to Broad Haven beach or extend the walk to Bosherston (see Walk 7). The onward route lies to the right. A short walk leads to Grassy Bridge, a causeway crossing the eastern branch of the ponds.

7 On the far side, turn right on a lakeside path, in time reaching Eight Arch Bridge.

41

8 Cross the bridge and follow a broad track over a low hill and on between fields that were once open as a deer park. Ignoring side paths, you will ultimately return to the car park at Stackpole Quay.

> ⓘ *Twelve species of bat have been recorded around the Stackpole estate, including the largest Welsh concentration of horseshoe bat*

– To shorten
The beach at Barafundle makes an ideal destination in itself (2.4km, 45min).

✚ To lengthen
Extend the walk along the southern arm of the lily ponds into Bosherston, where there is both a café and pub, adding 3km (1hr) (see Walk 7).

Stackpole Estate

Stackpole's origins date to Norman settlement under Elidur, one of William's knights who built a castle in the 12th century. By the end of the 17th century, the estate had passed to the Lorts and subsequently by marriage to the Campbells of Cawdor in Scotland, who made it their principal home. In 1735, they built Stackpole Court, which overlooked the head of the eastern valley for almost 200 years. However, the ravages of wartime requisition took their toll and, deprived of the estates that once supported it, the house became unviable and was demolished in 1963.

> ⓘ *One of the greatest delights in walking the Pembrokeshire coast is the sheer number of wildflowers to be seen in spring*

WALK 7
Bosherston Lily Ponds

Start/finish	*Bosherston Lily Ponds car park*
Locate	*SA71 5DW ///prouder.thumb.inhaled*
Cafés/pubs	*Café and pub nearby in Bosherston*
Transport	*Limited bus service from Pembroke Dock*
Parking	*National Trust car park at Bosherston (pay-and-display)*
Toilets	*At Bosherston Lily Ponds car park*

Time 1hr
Distance 3km (1¾ miles)
Climb 50m

A short walk around one of Bosherston's lily ponds

This short walk from Bosherston takes you around the western arm of Bosherston's three lakes, all of which are rich in wildlife and are best visited in June and July when the lilies are in flower. There is an opportunity to visit Broad Haven's fine beach, while the walk back along the southern shore of the lake is through verdant woodland. For those wanting a longer ramble, it can easily be tagged onto Walk 6.

The view up the western arm from the low hill

1 Follow the path from the bottom corner of the car park into a wood. At a junction bear left, following the lake shore to a **causeway** across the upper end of the western lake.

2 Cross the causeway to the opposite shore and follow the lakeside path right for 400m to a fork. Bear right climbing onto a low hilltop clearing overlooking the lake. After pausing to admire the view continue over the hill to rejoin the main path. Carry on, descending a flight of steps to reach a second **causeway**, this one crossing the foot of the central arm, which winds up the valley to the left. Over to the right, the three lakes converge at a dam above Broad Haven beach.

3 Reaching the far bank, the path swings right, following the bank to

WALK 7 – BOSHERSTON LILY PONDS

Looking up the central arm from the second causeway

yet another **causeway**. To incorporate Walk 6, go ahead at this point. Cross the causeway and carry on, the lake now hidden behind bushes and reeds. Before long, the way opens up to a view across sand dunes on the right. Stick with the main path, shortly reaching a waymarked junction.

4 Keep ahead, joining the Pembrokeshire Coast Path and walking a short distance to the outlet of the lakes behind **Broad Haven** beach.

5 There, turn right over a small bridge and follow the ongoing path back along

Budding lilies

the southern shore of the western lake. After crossing a bridge spanning a side creek, keep right, shortly passing an abandoned brick building and an old pump house that provided water for the nearby Castlemartin army camp. At a junction just beyond, go left back up to the car park.

> **+ To lengthen**
>
> Combine with Walk 6 to Stackpole Quay and return along the coast (11km, 3hr 45min).

Bosherston Ponds

The lakes were formed in the late 18th century by damming the three valleys converging behind Broad Haven beach. Sustained by freshwater springs and lime-rich water from the hills and surrounded by extensive woodland, they are a special wildlife environment, famous for a profusion of lilies and an abundance of wildlife throughout the year. Birds include heron, mute swan and several species of duck, whilst dragon and damselflies dart above the water. Go quietly and you might even see an otter.

Heading back along the western arm

WALK 8
St Govan's Head

Start/finish	Broad Haven Beach South car park
Locate	SA71 5DR ///rewarded.louder.sprinkle
Cafés/pubs	None on route
Transport	Limited bus service from Pembroke Dock
Parking	Car park at Broad Haven (pay-and-display) and St Govan's
Toilets	At Broad Haven Beach South car park
Military range	Access generally available at weekends, public holidays and some evenings, tel 01646 662280 or 662367 for information

Time 2½hr
Distance 7.5km (4¾ miles)
Climb 200m

Spectacular cliff formations and an unusual hermit's chapel will grab your attention on this scenic cliff-top walk

Although a there-and-back walk, there is plenty to see from the cliffs and the views on the return leg will appear completely different. Take care on the steep steps down to St Govan's Chapel and the rocky cove beyond. There is also shore access at New Quay and a path from the car park to the sands at Broad Haven. Check the Castlemartin range is open before beginning the walk.

New Quay

Looking back past the mouth of New Quay

WALK 8 – ST GOVAN'S HEAD

1 Leave the top of the car park through a gate beside the toilet block. A surfaced path leads down to Broad Haven beach. However, ignore that and take a path branching off right, which follows the top of the cliffs behind **Star Rock**. Keep going around the edge of a field to a gate marking the edge of the Castlemartin Range.

The Castlemartin artillery range covers some 6,000 acres of coast to Freshwater West. Since its requisition in 1938, it has been largely untouched by agriculture and the sheer abundance of wildflowers, insects and bird life is astounding.

2 Enter the range and follow the track as it cuts a broad swathe

SHORT WALKS PEMBROKESHIRE

Looking west towards St Govan's

through the rough gorse and bracken, but misses the views seen from a lesser path that winds closer to the top of the cliffs. Be careful, particularly with children, for the cliffs are sheer and the edge may be crumbling. Further on the separate ways combine. Look then for a track off left, which drops into a fold. At the bottom, the track to the left leads to a small beach at the head of a narrow cove, **New Quay**.

3 Head back up the track, and now ignore the junction, climbing to the head of the valley. At the top, go sharp left and follow the edge of Trevallen Downs out to **Long Matthew Point**. Carry on around the headland, turning again behind the old coastguard station on St Govan's Head and walk on above the cliffs to a car park at the end of the road above St Govan's Chapel.

WALK 8 – ST GOVAN'S HEAD

4 A flight of steps drops through a cleft to the tiny chapel. Pass through to find more steps that lead down to a small stone hive protecting **St Govan's Well**.

Legend says that the bell from St Govan's chapel was hidden from pirates within one of the boulders scattered about the beach, and if you strike the right one it will shatter to reveal the bell.

5 Climb back through the chapel to the top of the cliffs and retrace your outward steps to the car park at Broad Haven.

– To shorten

For a shorter walk of 4km (1hr 15min), cut straight across the neck of St Govan's Head bypassing Long Matthew Point.

St Govan's Chapel

St Govan's Chapel

St Govan is thought to have been an Irish abbot and contemporary of St David who, fleeing from pirates, took refuge in a cleft in the cliffs that miraculously opened. He subsequently remained here as a hermit until his death. The 13th-century chapel is supposedly built over his grave, while the fissure behind bears the imprint of his ribs. Two springs, one in the chapel and another on the beach are held to have curative properties.

WALK 9
The Green Bridge and Bullslaughter Bay

Start/finish	Stack Rocks car park
Locate	SA71 5HT ///racetrack.reverted.until
Cafés/pubs	None on route
Transport	Limited bus service from Pembroke Dock
Parking	Car park at Stack Rocks
Toilets	No public toilets available
Military range	Access generally available at weekends and public holidays, tel 01646 662280 or 662367 for information

Time 2¾hr
Distance 7km (4¼ miles)
Climb 120m

This exciting cliff-top, there-and-back ramble reveals some of Pembrokeshire's most stunning coastal features

A superb natural arch, amazing rock pinnacles and an awesome collapsed blowhole are just some of the sights along this short stretch of coast, and for those seeking a level walk, there is no climbing involved. Time your visit between May and July and you will see thousands of seabirds nesting on the cliffs. Check the Castlemartin range is open before beginning the walk.

The Green Bridge of Wales

SHORT WALKS PEMBROKESHIRE

Bullslaughter Bay from Mewsford Point

WALK 9 – THE GREEN BRIDGE AND BULLSLAUGHTER BAY

1 Leave the bottom end of the car park by the disabled spaces. Head half-right on a grass path towards the coast. There, a wooden platform provides a safe vantage from which to view one of Pembrokeshire's most spectacular coastal features, a magnificent natural arch known as the **Green Bridge of Wales**.

Perhaps Britain's most impressive natural arch, the Green Bridge is one of several along this coast. They are created by waves exploiting weaknesses in narrow headlands. As erosion continues, they eventually collapse leaving isolated pinnacles such as the Elegug Stacks.

2 Leaving the platform, follow the cliff path with the sea on your right past the Green Bridge to a small bay beyond, where there are the two

Elegug Stacks

impressive **Elegug Stacks**. Further on, beyond a stubby promontory, a narrow fissure cuts deep into the cliff. Carry on behind another small bay to discover the several rampart defences of a promontory fort. The headland they enclose has been much eroded with several caves and a massive, collapsed blowhole known as 'The Cauldron' or 'Devil's Punchbowl'.

> The abyss, known as The Cauldron, is open to the sea through a huge arch in its southern wall, and on the opposite side through narrow clefts to an inaccessible beach. Birds swoop through its portals to ride in the winds that are funnelled out through the top.

3 Continue along the cliff path behind Flimston Bay, where several more stacks rise above the boulder-strewn beach. There is another earthen-bank fort on Moody Nose before the path winds behind Bullslaughter Bay to **Mewsford Point**.

4 Simply turn around and retrace your steps back to the start.

WALK 9 – THE GREEN BRIDGE AND BULLSLAUGHTER BAY

Flimston Head

▬ To shorten
You must not go home without at least walking as far as The Cauldron (3km, 1hr).

ⓘ *Inland from Green Bridge is the medieval Flimston Chapel. Abandoned and used as farm buildings, it has been restored and again serves the local community*

Stack Rock Fort

WALK 10
West Angle

Start/finish	*West Angle Beach car park*
Locate	*SA71 5BE ///cascaded.shifting.laying*
Cafés/pubs	*Cafés at West Angle, Chapel Bay Fort and Angle Bay, pubs in Angle village and Angle Bay*
Transport	*Limited bus service from Pembroke Dock*
Parking	*Car park at West Angle*
Toilets	*At West Angle Beach car park*

Time 2hr
Distance 6km (3¾ miles)
Climb 90m

Amongst the attractions of this circular walk are a splendid beach, a restored Napoleonic fort and a waterside pub

West Angle Bay is a lovely, sheltered beach and from the headland, there is a fine view to Thorn Island and its fort. Another can be seen in the middle of the channel as you walk to Chapel Bay, where the fort has been opened as a museum. Further on, are Angle's present and original lifeboat stations before the way wanders back along the lane through the village.

Across Milford Haven to the LNG terminals

SHORT WALKS PEMBROKESHIRE

1 Begin along a gravel track from the top of the car park. After 200m, where it swings towards West Pill Farm, keep ahead and then almost immediately fork right with the Coast Path. The way runs on around the edge of fenced fields onto the promontory overlooking **Thorn Island** and its fort.

West Angle overlooks the entrance to the Milford Haven, a deep-water harbour that has been exploited as a fishing harbour, port for Irish and Atlantic trade, royal dockyards and terminal for the oil and LNG industries.

WALK 10 – WEST ANGLE

2 Continuing around the point, the view shifts along the Milford Haven estuary, where a second fort on Stack Rock guards the main channel. Beyond, jetties striding into the deep water provide berthing for massive tankers bringing oil and gas to the refineries and LNG terminal. Before long the path, now hedged, swings in past the landward defences of **Chapel Bay Fort**, finally coming out onto the end of a lane by its entrance.

3 Cross the lane and follow a track past the car park and a couple of cottages. Approaching a field entrance, bear left to continue with the Coast Path. After 1km, the scrub abates to

The original lifeboat station

reveal a view to the **Angle Lifeboat Station**.

4 Cross its access road to carry on with the Coast Path, shortly emerging in a meadow. Keep to the perimeter around the point, where a narrow gap in the hedge reveals steps to the rocky shore and the ruin of Angle's original lifeboat station.

5 At low tide you can stay with the shore to a pub and Cafe Môr, otherwise climb back and follow the field edge to the **Old Point House** pub.

6 Past the pub the ongoing track hugs the shoreline towards the head of the inlet, which can occasionally be flooded by very high tides. Fork left over a bridge and walk ahead to a junction at the edge of Angle.

7 Turn right past **St Andrew's Church** and continue through the village, where you will find the Hibernia Inn. It is then only another 1km back to the car park at West Angle beach.

> ⓘ *The modern lifeboat station is Angle's third, opened in 1992 to replace one built in 1927 to house Angle's first motorboat*

— To shorten

Leave the Coast Path at Chapel Bay Fort, follow its access track to the lane and go right back to the car park saving 3km (1hr).

Palmerston's Follies

The estuary's first defences were Tudor blockhouses, built to protect the narrow channel against the Spanish. Two and a half centuries later, the threat was from Napoleon, and the establishment in 1814 of a royal dockyard at Pembroke demanded new measures. In all twelve forts, a battery and a couple of 'Martello' towers were eventually built to defend the estuary. But, by the time they were finished, politics had shifted and the technology of warfare changed; they became known as Palmerston's Follies after the Prime Minister of the day. Today, only Chapel Bay Fort is open to visitors and houses a splendid museum.

The Old Point House

View from south-east tower towards the tidal mill

WALK 11
Carew Castle

Start/finish	*Carew Castle car park*
Locate	*SA70 8SN ///underway.collides.proved*
Cafés/pubs	*Pub in Carew and tea room at castle*
Transport	*Limited bus service from Pembroke Dock*
Parking	*Car parks at Carew Castle and Butts Lane*
Toilets	*Opposite Carew Castle car park*

Along quiet lanes and paths, this walk is ideal for a gentle evening stroll, but equally suitable for a full day out if you wander around both the impressive castle and restored tidal mill, perhaps stopping off at the Carew Inn for lunch. If the weather is fine, you might take along a picnic and enjoy the views of Carew River.

Time ½hr
Distance 1.5km (1 mile)
Climb 10m

Although the shortest walk in the book, there is a castle, mill and fine Celtic cross to see

Carew Castle from the lane

SHORT WALKS PEMBROKESHIRE

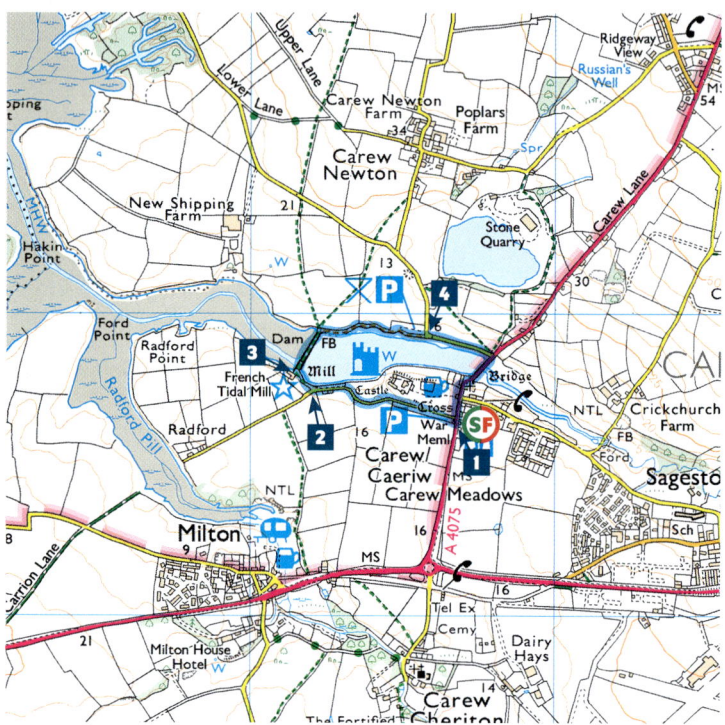

1 The entrance to the castle lies opposite the car park. Here you can buy a joint entry ticket for the castle and mill before starting out (both are administered by Cadw). The walk then follows the lane away from the main road past the imposing ruins of the **castle**.

The castle was founded in the 11th century by the Normans to consolidate their rule across South Wales. Over the centuries, the simple earthen defences evolved into a near-impregnable fortification before finally being slighted and eventually abandoned.

2 Eventually reaching a fork, bear right and carry on to the **tidal mill**.

The first mill was probably built to supply the castle, its wheel originally turned by the Carew

Carew Mill drive gear

River. By the early 17th century, the tidal barrage and sluices had been built, although the present mill building dates from the early 19th century.

3 The way then continues across the causeway dam, from which there is a lovely view back to the castle. The view is best seen when the mill pond is full, however, at low water, the Carew River is merely a meandering trickle. On the far bank follow the ongoing path to the right to another small **car park**.

4 Past the car park join the lane ahead back to the main road. Being mindful of traffic, turn right over the medieval bridge and carry on up the hill past the Celtic cross before finally turning into the car park. Take care as there is no footway on the last section opposite the Carew Inn, but when open, you can cut through the castle grounds.

Malacov Tower

WALK 12
St Ishmael's

Start/finish	St Ishmael's sports field
Locate	SA62 3TB ///edits.vesting.treatable
Cafés/pubs	Pub at St Ishmael's
Transport	No public transport
Parking	Lay-by next to sports field
Toilets	Next to sports field

Time 1½hr
Distance 4km (2½ miles)
Climb 100m

A sheltered coast, a secluded bay and a pretty, wooded valley all feature in this undemanding walk

After crossing fields from the tiny village of St Ishmael's, this easy walk follows an interesting section of coast above a succession of small bays, where there is a curious Victorian cliff-top folly. The return is along a pleasant, wooded valley to an ancient church and then follows lanes back to St Ishmael's, where there is a welcoming village pub.

Across Wenall Bay to Lindsway Bay

Flower-filled banks above Lindsway Bay

1 A signed path leaves the parking area beside the toilet block along the edge of the village sports field. At the top, turn right through the hedge and carry on by the boundary to emerge on the coast above a tiny cove at **Lindsway Bay**.

> Lindsway's claim to fame lies in a visit in 1955 by the Royal family, who disembarked from the Royal Yacht Britannica to picnic on the beach.

2 Follow the Coast Path to the right behind Longberry Point, undulating past a couple of larger bays to **Watch House Point**. There, hidden beside the path amongst the gorse and bramble are the remains of shelters that housed a wartime artillery installation protecting the approaches to Pembroke Dock. A little further along stands the impressive ruin of a tower, at first glance, a miniature medieval castle, but actually a Victorian folly. Known as the Malacov Tower, it is a monument to the Battle of Malakoff in the Crimean War. Beyond, the path winds down between curiously twisted trees to the tiny bay at **Monk Haven** where there is access to the shore.

> Used by traders, travellers and pilgrims, the Pembrokeshire coast is dotted with safe havens and sheltered landings such as this. Monk

Haven served St Ishmael's, whose original church may have been an early medieval monastic college.

3 Cross a bridge behind a high stone wall at the back of the stony beach to a signposted junction. There, turn right, leaving the Coast Path to follow a wooded path into the valley behind.

The valley was laid out as a pleasure garden for Trewarren House, which was built in 1845 for Gilbert Warren-Davis, one-time High Sheriff of Pembrokeshire. The wall across the head of the beach and a small boathouse were constructed at the same time.

4 Approaching a gate, go right again beside the boundary of Monk Haven Manor, soon coming out onto the corner of a track by **St Ishmael's Church**. Walk forward past the churchyard

St Ishmael's Church

and follow the ongoing track up to a junction.

5 There turn right, shortly reaching the village. Ignore the turn into Grove Road and carry on to a 'Y' junction. Just to the left is The Brook Inn, which serves food, but the way back lies to the right. Follow the lane through to the edge of the village and lay-by from which you began.

> ⓘ *Monk Haven looks to the Atlantic through the mouth of Milford Haven, a drowned valley, and one of the deepest natural harbours in the world*

WALK 13
The Dale Peninsula

Time 4hr
Distance 11km (6¾ miles)
Climb 340m

Start/finish	*Dale Beach car park*
Locate	*SA62 3RB ///enacts.quicksand.requiring*
Cafés/pubs	*Pubs and café in Dale*
Transport	*No public transport*
Parking	*Car park at Dale (pay-and-display)*
Toilets	*At Dale*

A longer, but relatively undemanding ramble, the effort repaid in stunning views and lovely beaches

Although a long walk with several ups and downs, there is nothing difficult along the way. After beginning along a lane, the route winds behind successive bays onto St Ann's Head. From there the path stays high along the western cliffs, passing behind a lighthouse before turning in above a generally deserted beach to return by way of fields and lane to Dale.

Dale

Descending to Westdale Bay

1 Out of the car park, turn right, keeping left at successive junctions to follow the coast road out of the village towards Dale Point. Eventually, some 150m beyond **Point House**, watch for the Coast Path leaving through a gate on the right.

2 Follow the Coast Path past Dale Fort, the undulating path curving behind Castlebeach Bay. After 400m, just after a footbridge at the head of the secluded bay, look for an ivy-clad lime kiln hidden beside the path. Before long the tall navigation beacon on **Watwick Point** comes into view. One of several beacons strategically placed to help shipping navigate the narrow, deep-water channel of Milford Haven.

3 Turning the point, the path continues above the cliffs, winding behind Watwick Bay where a path branches off down to the beach. The route, however, continues ahead, shortly reaching **West Blockhouse Point**. Almost hidden over to the left is another of Palmerston's forts, while three more navigation towers are ahead.

Map continues on page 77.

4 Cross the access track and follow the ongoing path past the emplacements of a gun battery, which was manned during the two world wars. Carry on around **Mill Bay**, the path eventually dropping to a small rocky beach at its head.

> In 1485 Henry Tudor landed here with a small band of supporters from France and just 15 days later, defeated Richard III at Bosworth to become Henry VII.

5 The path then climbs back onto the cliffs towards **St Ann's Head**, shortly passing between former coastguard cottages and a walled allotment. Carry on to more cottages behind the St Ann's Head lighthouse, continuing beside the fence to a gate by a small building housing a foghorn. Follow the drive away to the right past a converted lighthouse and on to the station boundary just past a set of cottages on the right.

6 Immediately beyond the station boundary wall, take a path off left to continue around the coast. Little Castle Point was the site of an Iron Age fort, and a little further on stood the now demolished buildings of HMS Harrier, a naval radar and meteorological school that closed in 1960. At **Great Castle Head** there are the embankments of another promontory fort, beyond which the path drops steeply behind Westdale Bay, where steps lead down to the beach.

WALK 13 – THE DALE PENINSULA

7 Leave the Coast Path above the beach through a gate on the right and strike across a field. Emerging onto a track, follow it forward past **Dale Castle** to the main lane and continue past the village church. After some 250m, look for a kissing gate on the right. Head to a gate opposite and follow a diagonal path to the road behind Dale's boatyard. Go left back to the car park.

> **— To shorten**
>
> For a shorter walk of 3km (1hr), reverse the route from Dale to Westdale Bay, where there is easy access to the beach.

The disused rear light on Dale Head

Lighthouses

Tradition holds that Henry VII built a chapel on St Ann's Head to commemorate his landing at Mill Bay. The tower served as a landmark for seafarers and a beacon would make it the oldest 'lighthouse' in Wales. The first dedicated light was installed as a commercial venture in the 17th century, but the enterprise folded because of the owner's dishonesty in collecting dues. In 1714, a pair of lights were built, whose alignment kept approaching vessels clear of Crow Rock to the south-east. The front light was re-sited in 1841 because of cliff erosion and remains in use as an automated station. The rear light was discontinued in 1910 and subsequently used as a coastguard lookout until 1993.

WALK 14
Runwayskiln and Marloes Sands

Start/finish	*Runwayskiln car park*
Locate	*SA62 3BH ///direction.mistaken.into*
Cafés/pubs	*Café in Runwayskiln*
Transport	*No public transport*
Parking	*National Trust car park at Runwayskiln (pay-and-display)*
Toilets	*No public toilets available*

A rewarding route that begins across fields past the Marloes Mere wetland reserve. At the coast are the impressive embankments of an Iron Age fort to explore before following the cliffs above Marloes Sands, from which there are splendid views to Gateholm and Skokholm Islands. There is then an opportunity to spend time on the beach before climbing back to the car park.

Time 1½hr
Distance 4km (2½ miles)
Climb 120m

Marloes Sands is one of Pembrokeshire's finest beaches and there is much to see along this cliff-top ramble

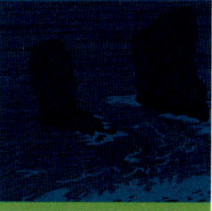

Above Marloes Sands back to Gateholme Island

1 Leave the bottom entrance of the car park by the information hut. At the junction just beyond, go sharp right along a hedged track to pass the Runwayskiln youth hostel. The track continues past the **Marloes Mere** reserve, later ending in a field. Keep ahead by the right margin, following it around to a small gate onto the Coast Path.

2 Just to the right is an impressive promontory fort occupying a slight headland between Victoria and Watery bays. After exploring, follow the coast back left to Horse Neck, a narrow

WALK 14 – RUNWAYSKILN AND MARLOES SANDS

Rock pools on Marloes Sands

peninsula that almost, but not quite, connects with **Gateholm Island**.

> The bay on the western side is known as Albion Sands, where low tide can reveal rusting scraps of ironwork. They are all that remain of the paddle steamer Albion, which ran aground in 1837. All the passengers and crew made it ashore.

3 Retrace your steps on Horse Neck to rejoin the Coast Path and continue along the cliff-top path above **Marloes Sands**, eventually dropping to a junction. The path to the right drops safely to the beach, where you might spend the rest of the day – but be wary of the tide.

4 The way back is to the left, a steady climb that eventually meets a lane. Go left back to the car park.

– To shorten
Reverse the route and just walk down to Marloes Sands (2.5km, 1hr).

ⓘ *Some 20 miles offshore and 41m high, the Smalls Lighthouse is the most remote in Britain. The light has a range of 18 miles*

Across Marloes Sands to Gateholme and distant Skomer Islands

Gateholm Island

Although barely separate from the land and only an island at high tide, Gateholm is geologically distinct from the cliffs behind, and is actually the same Old Red Sandstone rock formation as Skokholm Island and St Ann's Head. The island bears traces of early habitation, including what is thought to be the remains of an early Christian monastic community. The apparent path onto it can be dangerous and attempting to clamber up is not recommended.

WALK 15
Wooltack Point

Start/finish	Martin's Haven car park
Locate	SA62 3BJ ///puns.liberty.essay
Cafés/pubs	None on route
Transport	No public transport
Parking	Car park at Martin's Haven (pay-and-display)
Toilets	At Martin's Haven

Time 1¼hr
Distance 3km (2 miles)
Climb 100m

An easy short walk around South Pembrokeshire's most westerly point; a good spot to look for seals

Compact and surrounded by sea on three sides, the Deer Park peninsula almost feels like one of the small islands onto which it looks. There is an initial gentle climb to the lookout station at its highpoint before the path winds above a succession of tiny coves around its edge. There are small exhibitions about the area's wildlife and boat trips leave the beach at Martin's Haven to the nearby islands.

Martin's Haven

SHORT WALKS PEMBROKESHIRE

1 Out of the car park, walk to the left along the lane, passing the Lockley Lodge Visitor Centre. Here you can learn about the islands and their wildlife and even watch what is happening live on CCTV. Just beyond, the lane swings right past a small visitor centre and toilets to the small beach at **Martin's Haven**.

> Don't forget to look for a stone set into the wall and inscribed with a Celtic cross, suggesting the cove was a landing place for early Christians travelling from Ireland.

2 Return to the bend in the lane and now turn right through the gate into the walled enclosure of the Deer Park. Take the roughly stepped path, which rises ahead over an Iron Age defensive embankment that provided landward protection for a settlement on the headland. At the top of the steps, bear right and carry on climbing to the Coastguard **lookout station** at the top of the hill.

The lookout on the highpoint of Deer Park is manned by trained National Coastwatch Institution volunteers, who keep a weekend visual and radio watch for distress incidents along this stretch of coast.

3 The path continues beyond onto the tip of **Wooltack Point**.

4 Turn around and retrace your steps off the point, but then bear right to follow a path above the western cliffs – be careful not to get too close to the edge. The way meanders above a series of inaccessible rocky coves where seals sometimes pull out of the water, particularly in late summer when they have their pups.

Wooltack Point

5 When you reach a gate in the enclosure wall above **Renney Slip**, do not go through but instead go left beside the wall, strolling down to the gate passed through at the start. Turn out of the Deer Park and walk back to the car park.

— To shorten

Climb just as far as the lookout station for a view out to the islands (1km, 30min)

Deer Park

The Wooltack peninsula was once part of the Kensington estate, whose seat lay at St Brides, and was enclosed at the beginning of the 19th century. The title Deer Park is perhaps a pretentious misnomer as there is no record of deer ever having been kept, and indeed, encircled by sheer cliffs, would be an unsuitable place for a hunt. The stone wall parallels a ditch and bank fortification, which protected an Iron Age settlement on the promontory, the largest such fortification in Wales.

Celtic cross stone

USEFUL INFORMATION

Tourism bodies

Visit Pembrokeshire
www.visitpembrokeshire.com

Pembrokeshire Coast National Park
www.pcnpa.org.uk

Pembrokeshire County Council
www.pembrokeshire.gov.uk

The National Trust
www.nationaltrust.org.uk

Transport enquiries

Rural bus routes and timetables are liable to change, and it is essential to obtain up-to-date information from Pembrokeshire County Council

www.pembrokeshire.gov.uk/bus-routes-and-timetables

Transport
www.traveline.cymru

Thomas Taxis
tel 01834 812782

Range information

Access to Castlemartin Range East is generally available at weekends, public holidays and some evenings. Contact the Castlemartin Range Office
tel 01646 662280 or 662367

Accommodation

Plentiful accommodation in Pembrokeshire can be booked via
www.visitpembrokeshire.com/holiday-accommodation-search or direct.

© Dennis and Jan Kelsall 2024
First edition 2024
ISBN: 978 1 78631 175 7

Printed in Singapore by KHL printing on responsibly sourced paper.
A catalogue record for this book is available from the British Library.
© Crown copyright and database rights 2024 OS AC0000810376
All photographs are by the authors unless otherwise stated.

CICERONE

Cicerone Press, Juniper House, Murley Moss, Oxenholme Road,
Kendal, Cumbria, LA9 7RL

www.cicerone.co.uk

Updates to this Guide

While every effort is made to ensure the accuracy of guidebooks as they go to print, changes can occur during the lifetime of an edition. Any updates that we know of for this guide will be on the Cicerone website (www.cicerone.co.uk/1175/updates), so please check before planning your trip. We also advise that you check information about transport, accommodation and shops locally. We are always grateful for updates, sent by email to updates@cicerone.co.uk or by post to Cicerone, Juniper House, Murley Moss, Oxenholme Road, Kendal, LA9 7RL.

Register your book: To sign up to receive free updates, special offers and GPX files where available, register your book at www.cicerone.co.uk.